The Tourist Trophy

IN OLD PHOTOGRAPHS

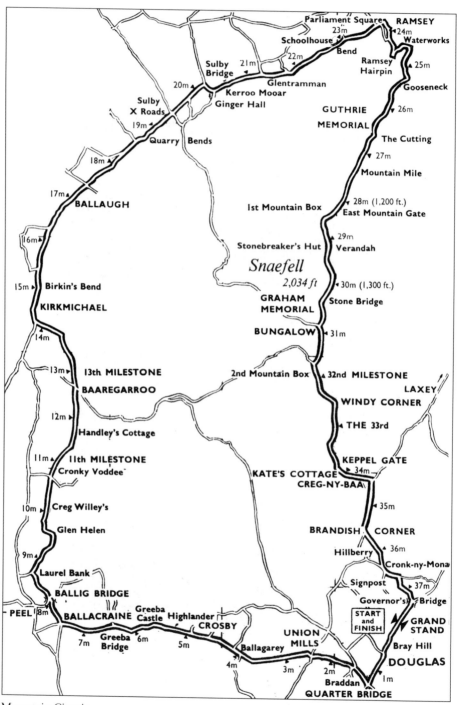

Mountain Circuit

The Tourist Trophy

IN OLD PHOTOGRAPHS

Collected by BILL SNELLING

Alan Sutton Publishing Limited
Phoenix Mill · Far Thrupp · Stroud
Gloucestershire

First published 1994

British Library Cataloguing in Publication Data

A catalogue record for this book is available from the British Library.

ISBN 0-7509-0635-9

Typeset in 9/10 Sabon.
Typesetting and origination by
Alan Sutton Publishing Limited.
Printed in Great Britain by
Redwood Books, Trowbridge.

The AJS workshop in Douglas, 1952. On the benches are a Porcupine 500 (No. 14) and a 7R 350, the standard model, not the works three valve.

Contents

Freddie Frith plunges down Bray Hill on the Senior works Norton, 1938. Two third places were his haul for the year, plus a share in both Junior and Senior manufacturers' team prizes.

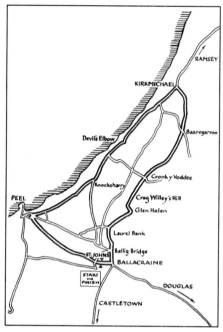

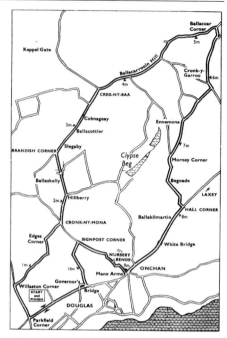

St John's Circuit   Clypse Circuit

Graham Walker puffs on a celebratory cigarette after a second place ride in the 1932 Lightweight TT on the four-valve Rudge. The young schoolboy admirer is his son Murray Walker who is now the well-known motor racing commentator.

6

Introduction

The Tourist Trophy

The Isle of Man TT races, which started in 1907, still deserve to be called 'the world's finest road races'. The thousands of riders and spectators who make their way to this small island in the Irish Sea each year in June from all over the world are positive proof of its enduring draw and international status.

When motorcycle racing started at the turn of the century in Europe, the emphasis was on sheer speed, and this bred 'monster' machines with large-capacity engines in minimal frames. These racing machines lacked any connection with the underpowered motor cycles that were being built for ordinary motorcyclists. So, in the TT's infancy, British manufacturers wanted races they could use to promote their road machines. The emphasis was not purely on all-out speed – the race regulations were framed to help develop the safer, faster, more manageable touring motor cycle which could be ridden by anyone, and hence the races were given the title of the Tourist Trophy. Each machine was required to have an efficient silencer, two brakes, mudguards and a toolbox. The tools were a necessity because of frequent stops to repair punctures caused by the many horseshoe nails on the roads, as well as broken valves and valve springs which were the result of metal technology that couldn't cope with the racing speeds of the bikes. There was even a fuel consumption restriction – single-cylinder machines had to average 90 mpg, multicylinders 75 mpg.

The pioneer machines very quickly mastered the 10 mile St John's circuit and a greater challenge was needed. This was provided by the 37¾ mile Mountain circuit which has been little changed since 1911, when the lap record was set at barely 50 mph. This speed seems slow by today's standards, but it is important to remember that the record was set on unmade roads and that the Mountain section was little more than a cart track with grass growing between the ruts.

As time passed, the circuit was improved. A few miles of tarmacadam were laid by 1922 and motorcycle technology moved on apace after its forced development during the First World War.

After the war manufacturers such as Rudge, Sunbeam, Velocette and Norton were in the happy position of being able to buy the services of the best riders and engineers in a frenzied pursuit of race victories that would translate into increased sales of their road machines. Foreign makers also sought to develop their machinery and to gain prestige by competing on the Isle of Man. Sometimes they brought their own riders such as Ewald Kluge (DKW) and George Meier (BMW) from Germany and the Italian Omobono Tenni (Moto Guzzi), but usually they enlisted the best British riders, such as Stanley Woods (Guzzi) and, after the Second World War, Geoff Duke (Gilera) and Mike Hailwood (Honda, MV, Ducati and Suzuki). This keen sense of competition between the outstanding riders and the leading manufacturers has continued to the present day.

The Amateur TT and the Manx Grand Prix

In 1921 the Auto Cycle Union, organizers of the TT races, had refused a request from the Manx Motor Cycle Club and others to hold a race for amateur riders during the TT meeting, and in 1922 they offered to hand the TT meeting over to Belgium, citing dissatisfaction with the course and problems caused by the Island's authorities over their strict Sunday observance laws. Faced with losing their major race meeting, the Manx MCC laid alternative plans for their own meeting, for privateers, to be held later in the year. The threat to the TT races died down, but by this time the Manx club had formulated their own rules and the first Amateur TT was run on 20 September 1923 as a single five-lap race with classes for standard 500 and 350 cc machines. The divisive 'amateur' regulations which gave so many problems up to 1929 were changed for 1930, at the insistence of the ACU, and the Manx Grand Prix was born. The simplified rules excluded only those riders who had ridden in specific International race meetings.

The races, held each year in September over the TT Mountain course, have proved to be an ideal training ground for British and Commonwealth riders who have gained valuable experience there before venturing into the TT. A win in the Manx Grand Prix at any time up to the 1950s would almost certainly have guaranteed either a works ride or works-assisted machinery for the following year's TT.

Multiple winners of the Manx Grand Prix are a thing of the past because winners of the main races are given an entry for the next year's TT meeting. Only in the Classic races for pre-1972 machinery, first held in 1983, are previous winners allowed to ride. But the list of road race champions and TT winners who started their Island career in the Manx Grand Prix is a long one, from Harold Daniell, Freddie Frith, Maurice Cann, Geoff Duke, Cromie McCandless, Bob McIntyre and Phil Read to Steve Hislop, Ian Lougher, Robert Dunlop and Philip McCallen.

The Tourist Trophy in Old Photographs is a journey through the history of motorcycle road racing, showing the men and machines that have made the TT meeting a landmark in the sport and a tradition that will shortly be celebrating its ninetieth birthday.

Acknowledgements

Many of the pictures in this book have been drawn from the Keig Collection, a twenty thousand plus archive of TT history which runs from 1911 to the 1970s. Copies of the Keig pictures can be obtained from S.R. Keig Ltd, 51 Strand Street, Douglas, Isle of Man, tel. (0624) 673111. I am very grateful to the following people who freely gave access to their private collections of TT photographs: Alan E. Kelly, Dave Masters, Dennis Corkill, Bob Dowty, Doug Davidson and Roy Cowin. I would also like to thank everyone else who helped me to compile this book.

Bill Snelling

SECTION ONE

The Tourist Trophy
1907–1939

Riders' line-up, 1905. Roads on the Isle of Man were used for racing even before the first TT. That year the English qualifying trials for the International race, to be held in Austria, took place on a 25 mile course in the south of the Island. The riders are, left to right: J.S. Campbell (Ariel, winner), W. Hodgkinson (JAP), -?-, G. Wilton (Barnes),-?-. Sir Arthur Conan Doyle, the creator of Sherlock Holmes, was an interested spectator, and entered T.H. Tessier on a Roc.

The flag drops and the very first TT is under way, 10 a.m. 28 May 1907. Frank Hulbert (No. 1) and Jack Marshall (No. 2) are both on 3½ hp Triumphs, entered by the factory. Marshall finished second and Hulbert third in the single-cylinder class. Marshall went one better the next year, winning in the same class.

H. Rembrandt Fowler (Norton), 1907. Fowler was the winner of the twin-cylinder class at the first TT in that year. He had to contend with punctures, plug changes and drive-belt repairs en route to victory. The Peugeot-engined Norton averaged 36.2 mph and over 90 mpg. Fowler was a private entrant but his mechanic was James L. Norton, founder of the famous firm which has won many TTs since 1907.

Unidentified competitor, Church Street, Peel, 1910. Peel was the only town encountered on the St John's course, which was used for the last time that year.

Winner Jack Marshall, 1908. This is what the well-dressed motorcyclist wore: a flying helmet, corduroy breeches and riding boots. A spare drive-belt is coiled up on the rear carrier. The toolbox would have held tools to change valves, which were prone to breaking, and tyre levers, to repair the inevitable punctures caused by horseshoe nails.

Jack Marshall (3½ hp Triumph), Douglas Corner, Kirk Michael, 1908. The road surface was cutting up as a result of the race – the 'racing line' shows a definite groove. With a single speed and no clutch, many competitors had to coast round this corner with the exhaust valve lifted, restarting on the drop down to Glen Wyllin.

A group of competitors gather for silencer and braking tests, prior to the TT, 1910. They include riders of BAT (Best After Test) and DOT (Devoid Of Trouble) machines. As the TT races were originally for touring machines, the road-going aspects of the bikes were tested, along with their speed and fuel consumption.

General view of the start line, 1910. A purpose-built scoreboard has replaced the original blackboard, which was borrowed from the local school. The majority of spectators would have arrived on horse-powered vehicles, some of which can be seen parked in the foreground. Their motive power would have been 'refuelled' in the stables, well away from the bikes.

Charlie Collier (Matchless), 1910. A son of the founder of the Matchless Motorcycle Co., Collier was victorious in the ten-lap (158 mile) race that year. This was the last year the short St John's course was used. Collier also won the 1907 single-cylinder class.

Competitors line up on the Quarter Bridge Road at the start of the first Mountain course TT, 1911. There were refuelling pits at Braddan Bridge and Parliament Square, Ramsey.

Freddie North (Ariel), 1911. North was a works trials rider. It is quite possible that this was the machine on which he won several gold medals in the Auto Cycle Union's six-day trials and other long-distance events.

D.C. Bolton (Rudge), Ramsey hairpin, Senior TT, 1912. Rudge won five TTs, but the Coventry-built machine was unlucky for Bolton on this occasion, when he had to retire.

H. Thornton (Douglas), 1913. Mechanical maladies and injuries sustained in the two-week practice period meant that many riders were non-starters. Thornton was just one of these. Similar machines to this one were used by despatch riders in the First World War.

T.E. Green (Rudge 'Multi'), 1913. This variable-geared model took A.R. Abbott to second place, but Green's machine failed to last the race.

Oliver Godfrey (Indian), starting in the Senior TT, 1914. The start line and pits were at the top of Bray Hill, approximately half a mile below today's start line.

The Braid brothers, Ossie and Ray, on Norton side valvers, 1914. As standard, their machines were single speeders, but the Braids added a variable-speed crankshaft pulley to assist with the mountain climb. Ossie finished forty-sixth, Ray fifty-first. Norton is the only manufacturer to have entered machines in virtually every TT meeting. The latest rotary-engined machine as ridden by Steve Hislop to win the 1992 Senior TT can reach almost 200 mph; the side valvers shown above would probably reach 75–80 mph.

Billy Newsome (Douglas) gives his pit a cheery wave as he starts another lap, 1914. The 1914 course missed out the Signpost Corner, Governor's Bridge section, bearing right at Cronk-ny-Mona, rejoining today's circuit at the top of Bray Hill.

Laurie Boston (NUT), Junior TT, May Hill, Ramsey, 1914. He retired in his only TT. The cryptic message is a reference to his nephew's passion for motor cycles, which led to his riding in the Manx GP. The Newcastle Upon Tyne (NUT) firm won the 1913 Junior TT, with rider Hugh Mason.

Tommy de la Hay (Sunbeam), 1914. De la Hay's solid allegiance to the Wolverhampton marque brought him victory in the Senior TT in 1920.

H.V. Colver (Matchless), 1914. Bert Colver, refuelling his low-slung V-twin in the pits, was on his way to fourth place after gearbox problems slowed him down. Many generations of his family worked at Matchless.

Oliver Godfrey (Indian), 1914. Godfrey, a TT pioneer, was the first rider to score an overseas success when he rode his American V-twin to victory in the 1911 Senior TT. He dead-heated in the 1914 Senior for second place with Howard Davies on a Sunbeam.

A weary Howard Davies (Sunbeam) after his dead-heat second place in the Senior, 1914. The Hutchinson company no longer makes tyres but still manufactures rubber hoses for the car industry.

Eric Williams (AJS), 1914. Williams won two Junior TTs, one each side of the First World War. The side valve featured a two-speed gearbox and a countershaft. Eric's second win was the 1921 Junior.

W.H. Longton (Alldays), 1914. With a wheelbase this long Longton must have had trouble getting his motor cycle round the Ramsey hairpin. (The Governor's Bridge section was still six years away.)

Vic Horsman (Norton), 1920. Horsman, world and British record breaker at Brooklands, was less successful in the TT. The BRS (Brooklands Racing Special) Norton failed to get him to the finish in the Senior TT that year.

Douggie Brown (Norton), 1920. Brown was the first Manxman to achieve a leaderboard place – he came second in the Senior TT. His brother George was instrumental in keeping the TT on the Island when the Auto Cycle Union offered the meeting to Belgium in 1922.

Nelson Sclater (Norton), 1920. That year Sclater was the only person to race a Manx-built motor cycle, the Aurora, in the Junior TT. Unfortunately it failed to complete a lap.

The start line, 1921. Up until 1934 competitors had to start the race with a stone-cold engine – not an easy task with monograde oils.

Stan Jones (Velocette), 1921. An accomplished trials rider, Jones's third place was the first top-three position for Velocette, the Birmingham firm. A Velocette – 'little Veloce' – two-stroke never won a TT. This was left to the overhead camshaft models introduced in 1925.

Stanley Woods (Cotton), 1922. This first ride was the start of a fabulous career for the Ulsterman. It was punctuated by the odd fall and a fire in the pits where the machine – and Stanley – caught fire, but despite these incidents Woods carried on to finish fifth.

C.M. Fairweather (Coulson), 1922. This machine features rear springing – the leaf spring can be seen just below the number-plate. There was no rear brake and the front brake wouldn't look out of place on a bicycle. What appears to be a toolbox on the tank is an extra oil tank, with a cable-operated plunger pump.

Jimmy Simpson (Scott), 1922. After this first ride Simpson rode every year through to 1934, when he finally won a TT – the Lightweight, on a Rudge.

C.W. 'Paddy' Johnston (New Imperial), 1922. Paddy's TT career spanned twenty-nine years, from this first ride through to sixteenth place in the 1951 125 cc race on a Sun.

Bert le Vack, with the 'double knocker' 350 cc JAP engine he developed fitted to his New Imperial, 1922. After leading and raising the lap record above the Senior figure, the gearbox seized.

Freddie Dixon (Indian), 1922. Dixon rode the red American Indian for four years. His ride that year ended in retirement with a burst front tyre, but he was to win both solo and Sidecar TTs in later years.

Douglas Davidson with the works single-cylinder Indian, 1922. In 1920 Davidson was the first rider to be timed at over 100 mph in Britain, at Brooklands.

J.A. Porter (New Gerrard), 1923. The starting procedure – flagging riders away at 10 second intervals – is still in use today.

J.A. 'Jock' Porter (No. 21), 1923. Porter was the first rider to win a TT – the 1923 Lightweight – on a machine of his own manufacture. The New Gerrard, built in Gayfield Square, Edinburgh, used a Blackburne engine.

Ray Braid (Triumph), 1923. This Ricardo-designed four-valve machine was more powerful than the 1914 Norton (page 17), but Braid retired from the race.

S. Ford (Matchless), 1923. What happened to Ford and his overhead camshaft Matchless is unknown, for he didn't figure in the starters for this race.

Ulsterman Jimmy Shaw (16H side-valve Norton), 1923. The tank-top box would have held spanners, plugs, valve springs, etc.

R.S. Short (Weatherell), 1923. Built in Billericay, Essex, the Weatherell competed in the races for only that year. The designer, R. Weatherell, found himself in financial straits during the TT and his machines were sold by the Island's bailiffs. One machine is still part of a private collection on the Island.

Kenneth Twemlow, 1924. It was a double celebration for the Twemlow family – Kenneth won the Junior race and his brother Eric won the Lightweight, each on New Imperial machines.

Harry Reed (single-cylinder DOT), 1924. The Sidecar TT was not universally welcomed by all manufacturers, but Reed, the founder of DOT, rode this outfit to second place. He won the 1908 twin-cylinder race, also on a DOT.

Vincent Naure (Douglas), 1925. Four Spaniards entered for the TT that year. Their arrival prompted an Island-wide search for a Spanish translator. Here Naure adopts a nonchalant pose through the Governor's Bridge dip, in contrast to the apprehensive look from his passenger, M. Canto.

Graham Walker and passenger Tommy Mahon (Sunbeam), Ramsey hairpin, 1925. They retired from this race but had taken second place in the first Sidecar TT in 1923.

The Scott team, Ramsey, 1925. Lodging in the north of the Island, these team members were allowed to start practice sessions from Parliament Square, along with the Douglas team. Others, who lodged in Peel, were allowed to start from Ballacraine.

It is difficult to tell if it is pleasure or pain on Len Parker's face as he crosses the line to win the Sidecar TT in 1925. Unlike Freddie Dixon's 1923 winning outfit (page 34), Parker's Douglas was fitted with a rigid sidecar.

Frank Longman and Leo Davenport (AJS), 1925. AJS was all-conquering in the Junior class through the early 1920s. Longman hitched one to a sidecar and took on the 500s in the 1925 Sidecar TT. He and Davenport finished fourth.

Freddie Dixon (Douglas), Ramsey hairpin, 1925. Passenger Walter Denny is pushing the lever forward, thus lowering the sidecar and letting it bank round the corner. Dixon, the winner of the first Sidecar TT in 1923, led the next two Sidecar races but failed to finish.

The Douglas team of riders, mechanics and machines at their Ramsey headquarters, 1925. The Bristol-built horizontally opposed twins had their best TT year in 1925. Manxman Tom Sheard won the Senior TT, Freddie Dixon the Sidecar race.

Rex Judd (Douglas), 1925. Judd was a prolific Brooklands record breaker on Norton and Velocette machines, but could not match those performances on the Island, finishing just once in six rides.

Ken Twemlow (HRD), 1926. The TT course still lacked a tarmacadam surface on the Mountain section at this time – it was still just a rutted unmade road.

Alec Bennett (Velocette, No. 5) shadows Wal Handley round Ramsey hairpin, Junior TT, 1926. Bennett's win by over 11 minutes from second-placed Jimmy Simpson (Norton) was the first TT victory for Velocette. Handley (Rex-Acme) finished a distant third. Using a similar overhead camshaft single-cylinder engine, Velocette won another seven Junior TTs – from 1928 (Bennett again) to 1949 (Freddie Frith).

Harold Willis, 1928. Willis was not only a brilliant development engineer for Velocette, but also a competent rider. In both 1927 and 1928 he finished second in the Junior TT. Willis is acknowledged as having designed the first positive-stop foot-change mechanism, making the hand-change gearbox redundant overnight.

Alec Bennett, 1928. Bennett has just won his second Junior TT in three years. Behind him stands Eugene Goodman, the designer of the cammy Velocette.

R.A. McDermid receives assistance to get his Norton back on two wheels, 1928. A touch too much throttle at Ramsey hairpin was the probable cause of this mishap.

Tommy Spann (overhead camshaft AJS), 1931. Some riders have a distinctive helmet, but Spann was instantly recognizable from his black and yellow striped wasp jersey. This motor cycle failed him in the Senior.

Johnny Lind, 1931. It was a Velocette policy to invite overseas riders of their machinery to ride the TT. One such was the South African Lind, who finished ninth in the Senior on his Junior model.

Guglielmo Sandri, 1931. Sandri's name failed to appear in the TT books because of this seemingly jinxed machine. After a spill in practice his NSU ride was taken by R. Parkinson, who then fell off the bike in the race.

Big man, little bike: Graham Walker dwarfs the 350 Rudge as he heaves it into life, 1932. Walker was to finish fifth. An accomplished solo and sidecar rider, his only TT win was the 1931 Lightweight race, in which he beat his much smaller team mates.

Leo Davenport (JAP powered New Imperial), 1932. Davenport was the first quarter-litre TT winner to average over 70 mph on this very standard-looking model.

Jimmy Guthrie pushes his Norton off for the Senior TT, 1932. The two 'commissars' to the left are fire brigade officers.

Stanley Woods (Norton), Governor's Bridge, 1932. Woods completed the Junior/Senior double and repeated the feat the following year.

HRH Prince George chatting to Wal Handley, 1932. The TT races received royal patronage for the first time that year. The twelfth milestone corner was renamed Handley's Corner after he crashed his Rudge there in the 1932 Senior TT.

Arthur 'Digger' Simcock with the Senior OEC, 1933. Australian Simcock was not the luckiest of riders, achieving just four finishes out of twelve rides.

Sid Gleave (four-valve Excelsior 'Mechanical Marvel') receiving the victor's bonus on winning the Lightweight race, 1933. Runner-up Charlie Dodson (New Imperial), behind, has to make do with a consolation chat with his mechanics.

Manuel Ghersi, 1933. Ghersi rode Guzzi, Bianchi and New Imperial machines. He took two sixth places, one on a Guzzi and one on a New Imperial.

Designer-manufacturer-rider Chris Tattershall (CTS – Chris Tattershall Special), 1933. He rode his own creations in various guises between 1931 and 1953.

Sweden's Gunnar Kalen (Husqvarna), 1934. Kalen was a team mate of Stanley Woods and Ernie Nott in the Senior. Their machines had to be rebuilt prior to the race after their lorry crashed en route to the TT. Woods was leading on the last lap, but then ran out of fuel. All three retired.

A prophetic smile from Jimmy Simpson, 1932. The 250 Rudge was to provide his only TT win. This man, the first to lap the Mountain course at 60, 70 and 80 mph, finally found a bike strong enough to last the race distance.

Scotland's Jimmy Guthrie (Norton), 1934. The mid-1930s saw riders of the calibre of Guthrie, Stanley Woods and Freddie Frith take TT honours for the Bracebridge Street, Birmingham firm.

Jimmy Guthrie cranks his Norton through Creg-ny-Baa on his way to a Junior/Senior double, 1934. The TT course has changed considerably in the sixty years since this photograph was taken, but this view is virtually the same today.

Jimmy Guthrie, Parliament Square, Junior TT, 1935. Guthrie was killed racing in Germany in 1937. The Guthrie Memorial, formerly called The Cutting, is where he retired in his last TT, the 1937 Senior. In a fourteen-year span from 1923 to his untimely death, Guthrie won six TTs, one on AJS, the rest on Nortons, together with another six leaderboard places. His birthplace, Hawick, can be seen from the Guthrie Memorial.

Works Norton line-up, 1935. Left to right: Johnny Duncan, Walter Rusk, Jimmy Guthrie, 'Crasher' White. But for Stanley Woods's brilliant riding of the Guzzi in the Senior TT, Nortons would have taken all leaderboard places. Duncan, Rusk and Guthrie won the manufacturers' team award for both Junior and Senior races, and, being members of the Birmingham MCC, won the Senior Club team award.

The flag falls and Jimmy Guthrie (Norton) is away for six high-speed laps, 1935. The race was a classic duel between Guthrie and Stanley Woods (Guzzi). The Norton camp expected Woods to make a second pit stop, but Woods rushed through without stopping to start his last lap, 26 seconds behind the Norton. Guthrie finished, then had to wait for Woods to come home, which he did 14 minutes and 56 seconds later, a win for Stanley Woods by the margin of 4 seconds.

Phil Vincent (far left) with the 1936 team of Vincent riders who included Jock West (on the bike), Manliff Barrington, Jock Forbes and Jack Williams.

A Spaniard riding a French machine in the Isle of Man, 1936. This truly international effort by Miguel Simo netted him twelfth place in the Lightweight race. In subsequent rides on the Terrot he failed to finish.

Stanley Woods (DKW), 1936. Stanley's only TT on a German machine ended in retirement, but he set a new lap record, adding 2 mph – the first sub-30 minute Lightweight lap.

Freddie Frith, 1936. Following a win and second place in the 1935 Manx Grand Prix, Frith was given a works Norton contract for the TT the following year. The result was a win in the Junior followed by third place in the Senior.

Stanley Woods (Velocette), second in the Senior, 1936. Despite winning eight Junior races, Velocette was never able to win the Senior. Stanley finished second each year between 1936 and 1938 on the bigger Veloce single.

David Whitworth (Cotton) on his TT debut, 1937. The Gloucester factory always made its frames from straight tubes. The large and ungainly petrol tank is a 'TT special', fitted to try for a non-stop race.

Austrian F. Faltner rode this Belgian Sarolea into twenty-third place in the Junior in 1937.

Noel Pope (Norton), 1937. Pope holds the Brooklands solo and sidecar records in perpetuity after the track closed in 1939. This Senior ride netted him ninth place.

No mean competitor on two wheels, F.W.R. England (Cotton) retired in his only TT in 1937. 'Lofty' switched from two wheels to four as competition manager for Jaguar, his team winning Le Mans many times with the D-type.

O. TENNI GUZZI WINNER

Italian Omobono Tenni (Guzzi) was the first foreign national to win the Lightweight TT in 1937. He only finished twice on the Island – this win and a ninth place in the 1949 Senior TT. When he was leading the latter race a piston failed on the V-twin and he finished a lowly ninth on one piston, but he set the fastest lap earlier in the race.

BMW teamsters Karl Gall (No. 28) and George Meier (No. 9) head for practice, 1938. Gall failed to start after a road crash. Meier's race lasted barely a mile – a plug went duff on the line, then snapped in the cylinder head when he went to change it.

Karl Gall (BMW), 1938. A road crash kept Gall from the race, and he was to crash again at Ballaugh Bridge in practice for the 1939 Senior, sustaining fatal injuries. There is a memorial plaque to him on the wall opposite the Raven Hotel, Ballaugh.

The pre-war DKW, *c.* 1938. This was reputed to be the noisiest machine round the TT course. It is said that the screaming two-stroke could be heard over the water in Lancashire.

Harley Deschamps (Norton), 1939. In this, his only TT, Deschamps spilled at Laurel Bank. His machine was rediscovered recently and rebuilt, and now takes pride of place in the bar at the Crosby Hotel on the TT course.

Stanley Woods (Velocette), 1939. Keeping an impeccably tight line, Woods is completing his last TT race, the 1939 Senior. He came in fourth. He rode the same motor cycle in the Classic Lap of Honour in 1980, fifty-nine years after his first TT race.

Wilhelm Herz on a supercharged NSU 350 twin, 1939. Herz is looking the wrong way for the opposition – the NSU machines did not make the grade, all three entries retiring.

George Rowley (AJS), 1939. The supercharged V-4, full of tremendous but unfulfilled potential, was specifically built to challenge the BMWs. The machine did not start the race and supercharging was banned for racers after the Second World War. Rowley rode nineteen TTs, always on an AJS.

Harold Daniell (Norton), 1939. Norton were too busy on war projects to provide new machines for the TT in 1939, so Daniell was loaned this 1938 machine. On this Junior model he finished second to Stanley Woods (Velocette), setting the fastest lap.

Jock West (BMW), Quarter Bridge, 1939. The supercharged BMW twins were almost unbeatable in their 1939 form. West finished second to George Meier.

SECTION TWO
The Tourist Trophy
1947–1971

Manliff Barrington (Guzzi), Hillberry, 1947. When the TT restarted after the Second World War, in 1947, pre-war aces made all the running. Barrington was victorious in the Lightweight that year.

Manxman Jack Cannell (Clubmans Triumph), 1947. Practice times indicated he was a candidate for honours, but a fractured fuel line dropped Cannell down the list. Bill McVeigh (Triumph, No. 2) was the winner of the Lightweight Clubman race.

Jock West (AJS), 1947. After being thrashed by BMW in the last pre-war TT, AJS worked through the war years to combat the German threat. After supercharging was banned, the Porcupine racer was redesigned for its debut in 1947.

Mersey river pilot Harold Kirby (Excelsior), Lightweight TT, 1947. Kirby flirts with the bank at the Gooseneck, a favourite vantage point.

Freddie Frith (Guzzi), 1947. The record books show that Frith only rode British machinery in the TT, but that year he was due to ride this Italian machine in the Senior. A practice crash put him out of the race. In 1949 Frith was awarded the OBE for his racing successes.

Vic Willoughby (Mk VIII KTT Velocette), 1948. Technical editor of *Motor Cycle* magazine, Willoughby's expert writing made for interesting reading as he rode most of the works machines.

Bertie Rowell (Ariel square four), 1948. The travelling marshals have been an essential part of the TT for many years, with their ability to travel to incidents and to check that the course is clear before racing commences.

Sid Milne (350 cc split-single EMC), 1948. The EMC was not a bestseller in its day, and Milne rode this machine in three Clubman races without success.

Omobono Tenni (Guzzi), Ballacraine, 1948. Tenni finished ninth in the Senior, eleven years after winning the Lightweight race, also on a Guzzi.

Don Crossley (Triumph T100, No. 94) and F. Fairbairn (Vincent Rapide, No. 95) crank their machines into life for the 1948 Senior Clubman TT.

Ramsey baker Don Crossley keeps his Triumph on an even keel as he flies Ballaugh Bridge in the Senior Clubman, 1948. This race must have been good practice as that year Crossley won the Senior Manx GP on a Triumph. He also won the 1950 Junior on an AJS.

Spectators in the packed grandstand watch the start of the Lightweight race, 1948. The superiority of the Guzzi can be judged by the fact that Maurice Cann won by over 10 minutes from second man Roland Pike (Rudge). In third place Doug Beasley was a further 14 minutes behind.

This scene was captured less than a minute after the previous view. Dario Ambrosini (Benelli) leads, with the field well strung out behind him.

Harold Daniell (Norton, No. 89) nips inside Guy Newman (AJS, No. 78), Quarter Bridge, Junior race, 1948. Daniell's TT victories spanned the war years – he won the 1938 Senior, then repeated his success ten years later at a slower average speed because he used inferior 'pool' petrol.

George Brown (1000 cc Vincent) body-leans into Quarter Bridge, 1948. A works tester for the Stevenage firm, Brown led the 1000 cc Clubman TT until the last lap.

The effort of man-handling 500 lb of fuelless Vincent shows as George Brown is helped away after pushing his Black Shadow to a finish in the 1000 cc Clubman of 1948.

Jock West (AJS Porcupine) flies at Ballagaraghyn, just before Ballacraine, 1948. The jump has long since disappeared.

Bob Foster (Guzzi), 1949. Foster, like Stanley Woods and Freddie Frith before him, was another Velocette rider to try for TT victory with the Guzzi V-twin, but without success.

Geoff Duke (International Norton), Quarter Bridge, 1949. Duke was at the start of a career that was to make him a household name in the 1950s. He won the 1949 Senior Clubman race on this motor cycle. The machine is often exhibited at classic bike shows.

Hopwood's Junior model, 1949. Royal Enfield is better known for its trials machines, but the company did produce this cobby-looking Bullet model for the Clubman races.

Lightweight race-winner Manliff Barrington (Guzzi) reaches for a handkerchief to clean his face, 1949. Runner-up Tommy Wood (Guzzi) has yet to remove his helmet. These riders finished only 12 seconds apart, but 14 minutes ahead of Roland Pike (Rudge), who came third.

Les Graham (AJS), Cronk-ny-Mona, 1949. It was at this very spot on the last lap, when leading by 90 seconds, that the magneto drive sheared and Graham had to push home, finishing tenth.

A.A.F. Burton (Douglas), 1950. The model name – 90 Plus – represented the top speed of the Bristol-built flat-twin, which was not competitive against the 100 mph plus of the Norton and BSA machinery.

Rod Organ (Rapide), 1950. A 1000 cc Clubman race was included in the TT programme for three years and was a Vincent benefit, with each of the top three places taken by the V-twins. Organ is an artist who captures the spirit of the TT in his many paintings.

Junior Clubman race, 1950. Regulations for the early Clubman races for production machines insisted on a 'cold-engine' start, which contributed to this start-line chaos.

Dario Ambrosini (Benelli), 1950.

Bob Foster (Guzzi) flies on his way to Braddan Bridge, 1950. Foster suffered mechanical problems in this race and retired. The V-twin only won one TT – the 1935 Senior, ridden by Stanley Woods.

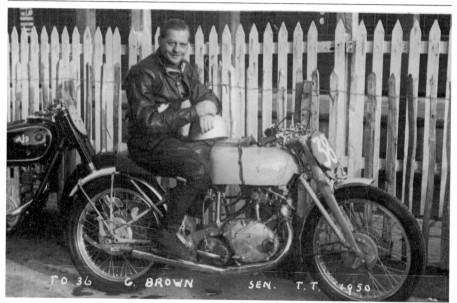

George Brown (Vincent), 1950. Brown was entered on the Grey Flash, but earlier injuries forced his withdrawal. He retired from racing after hitting the wreckage of Les Graham's fatal accident on Bray Hill in 1953, but carried on breaking world sprint records on his Vincents 'Nero' and 'Super Nero'.

Italian aggression exemplified as Dario Ambrosini heads for the winning line in the Lightweight TT, 1950. The machine was very similar to the one that took Ted Mellors to victory eleven years earlier.

Among the thronging crowd is Dario Ambrosini, receiving the plaudits and attention of the world's press after his winning Lightweight ride of 1950.

Artie Bell and Johnny Lockett (Nortons) compare notes about their works machines, 1950. They finished second and third to Geoff Duke in the Senior. The Mountain road was used (unofficially) by racers outside of practice times to test their motor cycles.

J.S. Bulto (125 cc single-cylinder Montesa), 1951. The TT has attracted many Spanish riders, but that year saw the first Spanish machine compete. Bulto finished fifth. He later made his own motor cycles – Bultaco – and won the 250 Production TT in 1967, when the rider was Bill Smith.

One, two, three for the works Nortons in the Junior TT, 1951. Geoff Duke (No. 48) won, backed up by Johnny Lockett (No. 68) in second and Jack Brett (No. 5) third. Duke set the first 90 mph Junior lap to win 3 minutes ahead of his team mates.

Geoff Duke apexes Governor's Bridge in the Senior, 1951. Duke achieved the Junior/Senior double that year, winning four TT races for Norton before leaving to join Gilera.

The Norton team for the Senior, 1951. Left to right: Johnny Lockett, Dickie Dale, Geoff Duke. Duke carries the number one plate by virtue of his win in the 1950 Senior.

Local rider Michael McGeagh (BSA) approaching Quarter Bridge, 1951. Taking over the ride at short notice, McGeagh suffered gearbox problems and completed the three laps stuck in third gear.

An unidentified rider tests the efficiency of his helmet as he drops his AJS 7R on the approach to Signpost Corner, *c.* 1951. The following rider seems a bit unsure about which direction bike and rider are heading.

Geoff Duke settles into the saddle at the start of the Senior, 1951. He won the Clubman Senior in 1949, followed it in the same year by a win in the Senior Manx Grand Prix, and then took the TT victory – a unique treble in motorcycling history.

The 125 cc Mondials, which were placed first, second and third in the first Ultra Lightweight TT, being swung ashore, 1951. Before the advent of roll-on, roll-off ferries, all machines, roadsters and racers, had to be craned off the Isle of Man Steam Packet ferries.

A clean sweep for Mondial in the Ultra Lightweight race, 1951. Cromie McCandless (No. 62) won from Carlo Ubbiali (No. 71) and Gianni Leoni (No. 66).

Bob McIntyre (BSA), 1952. McIntyre's first Island race was the Junior Clubman, in which he came second. Winning the Junior Manx GP the same year, he finished runner-up in the Senior with the same 350 cc AJS.

Reg Armstrong, Hillberry, 1952. The primary chain of Armstrong's works Norton was to snap right on the finish line as he won the Senior TT.

Reg Armstrong (Norton, No. 15), flanked by Ray Amm (Norton, No. 28), who came third, and runner-up Les Graham (MV, No. 17), 1952. Between Armstrong and Graham is Geoff Duke, who retired from the lead with clutch problems.

Les Graham (500 MV), 1953. After winning the Ultra Lightweight TT on the single-cylinder MV the day before, Les was killed in a second-lap accident on Bray Hill in the Senior.

Aircraft technician American Nick Nicholson (500 Manx Norton), 1953. Most manufacturers made batches of machines for the TT, also providing technical support with mechanics during the race period.

New Zealander Rod Coleman (AJS), Braddan Bridge, 1953. Coleman retired that year but came back to win the 1954 Junior on the AJS 7R3.

Ray Amm (350 cc Norton 'Kneeler'), Cronk ny Mona, 1953. This motor cycle was designed by Rex McCandless as a progression to his Featherbed frame. South African Amm tried the machine in practice, but reverted to a standard model for the race.

L. Turner drops his Excelsior at Quarter Bridge on the first lap of the Lightweight TT, barely a mile from the start of the race, 1953. This was his only TT ride. Cold tyres, a full tank and an overdose of adrenalin make this spectacle a not uncommon sight.

Werner Haas (NSU), 1953. Haas came second in the Lightweight race on the double-knocker twin.

Ray Amm, Senior race, Governor's Bridge, 1953. Amm won both the Junior and the Senior that year.

Geoff Duke (Gilera), 1953. This was Duke's first TT on the Gilera. It was not to be a winning debut – Duke slid off at Quarter Bridge, damaging the petrol tank.

Ray Amm (No. 61) receives an appropriate reward from his wife, Jill, for winning the Senior, 1953. The team boss, Joe Craig, is more interested in checking the fuel consumption. Amm fell off on the last lap but remounted to win by 12 seconds from Jack Brett (Norton, No. 20).

A rain-spattered Moto Guzzi single in the paddock, 1954. Guzzi built lightness into all of its racing machines. The horizontal-cylinder engine was first used in 1921.

Lightweight winner Werner Haas poses for the camera while Senior victor, Ray Amm (Norton No. 93), checks out the NSU, 1954.

The AJS three-valve 7R ridden by Rod Coleman to victory in the Junior, 1954. This was AJS's first TT win since 1922. The bulbous petrol tank served as a form of streamlining.

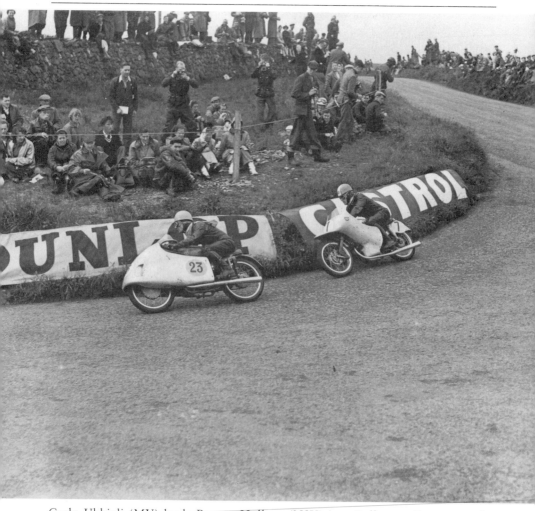

Carlo Ubbiali (MV) leads Rupert Hollaus (NSU) into Ballacoar Corner on the Clypse course, 1954. The race-leaders were never more than a few seconds apart during the whole race after a massed start. Victory went to Hollaus by a scant 4 seconds from Ubbiali.

Eric Oliver and Les Nutt (Norton-Watsonian), Nursery Bends, 1954. These men were victors of the first Sidecar TT since 1925. This machine used the Norton 'Kneeler' chassis, ridden solo in practice the year before by Ray Amm (p. 88). The 'Kneeler' was universally adopted for sidecar racing after Oliver's victory.

John Surtees (Norton), Signpost Corner, 1954. Surtees took eleventh and fifteenth places that year before commencing a career with MV, which resulted in four Senior and two Junior victories. He then turned to car racing.

Ray Amm (Norton) flies over what is now called Ago's Leap, Quarter Bridge Road, 1954. The fairing, with its extended nose, was unique to the works Norton. The picture epitomizes the road racing aspect of the Island, riders hurtling through town streets at speeds in excess of 160 mph. There is no chance of a lie-in for residents in practice week – morning practice starts at 5.30 a.m.

Ray Amm ('proboscis' Norton), 1954.

The sidecar field streaks away from the start to turn right at Parkfield Corner on the Clypse course, 1955.

Geoff Duke and wife celebrate his Senior TT win, 1955. To Duke's right is Giovanni Fumigalli, a long-time Gilera chief mechanic who attended his machinery right through his Gilera years.

The Italian domination of the front row of the grid was mirrored in the finishing order in this 125 race of 1955. Carlo Ubbiali (MV, No. 9) won from Luigi Taveri (MV, No. 4) and Guido Lattanzi (Mondial, No. 15). The other riders include Bill Lomas (MV, No. 1) and Umberto Masetti (MV, No. 18).

Scoreboard showing the details of the Ultra Lightweight TT, 1955. Luigi Taveri (MV No. 4) was the initial leader, then Carlo Ubbiali (MV) took over. Taveri regained the lead on the penultimate lap, but Ubbiali won by 2 seconds. Lattanzi (Mondial) held a race-long solitary third place.

With dark goggles as a precaution against the low evening sun, Ken Kavanagh sets out on his Junior Guzzi, 1955.

The BBC's Graham Walker, commentating from the radio shack at the top of the old TT grandstand, 1956. For many years the voice of the TT, Walker rode twenty-three races – solo and sidecar.

Horst Kassner steers a cautious path in a wet and windy Lightweight TT, 1956. The German NSU Sports-Max rider finished fourth in this, his only TT race.

Cecil Sandford (Junior DKW) skirts the advert-bedecked wall on the exit to Governor's Bridge, 1956. He finished fourth in the last appearance on the Island of the three-cylinder two-stroke.

John Surtees (500 MV), 1956. Surtees won the first of six Senior TT victories on his second-string MV, having damaged his number one bike when he hit a cow on Creg Willies Hill in practice.

Walter Zeller (BMW) accelerates from the pits, Senior TT, 1956. He finished fourth. The German machines did not repeat their pre-war solo success, but were to prove almost invincible in the sidecar class.

Pip Harris and Ray Campbell (Norton) about to take second place in the Sidecar TT, 1956. Fritz Hillebrand (BMW) came first.

Walther Schneider and Hans Strauss, 1956. This pair suffered their only TT retirement when this BMW outfit failed to finish.

Bill Boddice and Bill Canning (Manx Norton-Watsonian), Nursery Bends, 1957. Boddice's best result was a second in the 1955 race. His son Mick has won nine TTs.

Carlo Ubbiali leads Luigi Taveri (125 MVs), Parkfield, 1957. They finished second and third behind Tarquinio Provini (Mondial).

A.H. Mustard (Gold Star BSA), 1957. After the works bikes appeared with full 'dustbin' enclosures, a number of British privateers copied the design. In the background Sam Huggett of the Auto Cycle Union is conducting a helmet inspection.

Tarquinio Provini (250 Mondial), Governor's Bridge, 1957. The loop road was not used for the Clypse course.

Ulsterman Sammy Miller (Mondial), 1957. Miller took fourth place in the 125 race, but crashed while challenging for the lead in the 250 race, pushing in to finish fifth. Full fairings were outlawed after 1957 on safety grounds.

V-8 power: Dickie Dale (Guzzi), 1957. Dale finished fourth, despite only running on seven cylinders for most of the race. The bike was just proving its potential when Guzzi, along with Gilera and Mondial withdrew from racing at the end of 1957.

Australian Keith Campbell (Guzzi), 1957. Campbell finished second in the Junior race.

Deputizing for the injured Geoff Duke, Bob McIntyre (Gilera) accelerates out of Governor's Bridge, heading for the chequered flag and a win in the Junior TT, 1957.

Bob McIntyre (Gilera), Senior race, Quarter Bridge, 1957. This was his second TT win of Jubilee week. He was the first to lap the 37¾ mile course at over 100 mph.

John Surtees (MV four), Senior race, Quarter Bridge, 1959. Surtees won this race and went on to become the only man to win world championships on both two and four wheels.

Jackie Beeton and Eddie Bulgin (BMW), 1960.

Michio Ichino (Suzuki), 1960. This was the debut year for Suzuki, but the entry form listed the model name 'Colleda' instead of the make, which causes great confusion in TT history. Ichino finished sixteenth.

John Hartle (MV) pushes off from his pit stop to start the fourth lap of the Senior, 1960. The scoreboard has remained substantially unchanged since it was first used in the 1920s.

Bob McIntyre was still a leaderboard man, even when back on singles in 1961. He finished second in the Senior. He said that for 1961 he had a fast 250 (Honda), a slower 350 (Bianchi) and an even slower 500 (Norton), but it was only the Norton that finished.

Charlie Freeman and Billie Nelson raise doubt about the stability of a sidecar, 1961. Their Norton outfit clipped the bank at the Gooseneck and turned turtle. Nelson's head can be seen in the lower right of the picture.

Mike Hailwood (EMC), 1962. Hailwood strove to catch the all-conquering Hondas on Dr Joe Ehrlich's British-built 125. He held a leaderboard place but retired with engine trouble.

Ernst Degner ducks down behind the fairing of the 50 cc Suzuki to cut wind resistance, 1962. Degner led the East German MZ team for many years, before defecting to Japan and Suzuki in 1961, taking with him many years of two-stroke technology, which helped the Japanese firm to dominate small-capacity racing. The defection plans were hatched in a Douglas hotel during TT week. Degner had gone there ostensibly to listen to a jazz band, but was courted by the Suzuki team manager. Prior to this Suzuki had lagged behind the MZs and the four-stroke Hondas.

Florian Camathias (BMW), 1962. On one occasion his race transporter broke down en route to the TT. Undaunted, he unloaded the outfit and rode it up to Liverpool – the sound of the booming BMW in the Mersey Tunnel must have been amazing.

The East German Kreidler team line up for the first 50 cc TT, 1962. Left to right: W. Gedlich (No. 9) Hans Georg Anscheidt (No. 6) and Jan Huberts (No. 24).

Mike Hailwood (Benelli), Governor's Bridge, 1962. Hailwood had stopped to remove the streamlining earlier in the race.

Kunimitsu Takahashi (125 Honda), Quarter Bridge, 1962.

Chris Vincent and Eric Bliss (BSA twin), 1962. They pulled off an unexpected win in the Sidecar race after all of the fancied BMW riders had retired.

They look like giants, but these riders are the waif-like leaderboard men from the 50 cc race of 1962. Ernst Degner (centre) won Suzuki's first TT from Honda riders Luigi Taveri (left) and Tommy Robb (right).

Alberto Pagani (250 Crooks Suzuki) speeds past the Highlander Inn in the 1971 Lightweight TT.

SECTION THREE

The Amateur TT and the Manx Grand Prix

Les Randles (Sunbeam), 1924. Randles won the Amateur TT, his second successive win on this motor cycle.

P.B. Cheston (Blackburne-engined Chater Lea), 1924. Cheston was a retirement, having finished twenty-fourth the previous year on a Scott.

W.S. Empsall (Velocette) approaches Parliament Square, 1926. This motor cycle was the first private cammy Velo to race on the Island. Empsall won the 350 cc class, finishing eighth overall.

Bertie Rowell (Velocette), MGP, 1932. The front wheel pawing the air is indicative of a poor road surface, not power. Rowell and his brother Harold, both leaderboard men in the Manx, rode as extras in George Formby's classic TT film *No Limit*.

Austin Munks (Velocette, No. 64) nips inside Jim Swanton (New Imperial) in the Manx, 1934. The MGP attracts a smaller crowd than the TT, but there is no shortage of close racing from full-entry grids.

J.H. 'Crasher' White (Norton) leaps over the Union Mills railway bridge, Junior Manx, 1934.

An unidentified rider stoops to pick up the pieces after crashing at Parliament Square, Ramsey, 1936.

Wakefield's Dennis Parkinson, Junior MGP, 1948. Parkinson had a winning habit at the Manx – from 1932 to 1953 he won five Manxs – and he added a further win in the 1947 Junior Clubman TT on a Norton.

Ernie Lyons (Triumph), 1948. Lyons rode this experimental model to victory in the Senior MGP that year. The machine was built by the competition section at Meriden. It is said that Edward Turner, the boss of Triumph, was unaware of his factory's connection with the bike until after the race.

Thame's Ralph Seymour (Mk VIII KTT Velocette), 1948. First as a rider, then as a rider-dealer, Seymour rode and supported many riders through the years on his Velocette and Norton machines.

Geoff Duke (No. 23) and Cromie McCandless (No. 2), 1949. These men shared the honours at the Manx that year – Geoff won the Senior with Cromie second, and these positions were reversed for the Junior. Francis Beart (in beret and sunglasses) was the tuner of the McCandless Norton.

Bob Anderson (Norton), Quarter Bridge, 1956. Anderson is on his way to second place in the Senior MGP. After a motorcycling career that included two second places in the TT, Anderson turned to cars, racing MacLarens.

C.V. Bennett (OEC Atlanta), pushing into Parliament Square, 1925. More development work was required on this pre-production machine and Bennett failed to finish.

A split second from disaster, 1923. Harry Langman (Scott) was leading the inaugural Sidecar TT from Freddie Dixon (Douglas) by a wide margin – he only had to sit behind Dixon to take the win, but chose to pass him and forge ahead. At Braddan Bridge his enthusiasm caused him to flip the outfit, handing the race to Dixon. This picture was taken a split second before he hit his passenger Eddie Mainwaring against the bridge which caused the outfit to somersault across the road. Dixon, who can be seen just behind, had to take avoiding action. A recently found cine film shows the start of the action, but cuts off before the main prang.